FLIGHT

Shady Cosgrove

FLIGHT

Tiger, Flower, Coin

Covid came on me: an infection of spirit. First, I could hear it in my blood—Bengal tigers running through my veins. Take-home tests, even PCRs, all negative but still, that internal weight of feline haunch. Relief when the positive text message pinged in the middle of the night, and the virus, as though spurred on by acknowledgement, came in bursts—angry flowers in my chest—then resting, until it lodged in my throat like a coin. I couldn't swallow, couldn't speak for myself except to shout but no one listens to a shouting woman. Now I'm dizzy and hungry but uninterested in eating, as if the effort of food and joy is too much on a planet that is itself suffering an infection of spirit.

Immigrant Allegiance

Middle of the pandemic and America wants feedback on her poems—spams my inbox with drafts, live streams long-form rants. And just when I'm getting used to her, she ghosts quiet. Maybe it's the time difference, she could be sleeping, I tell myself. Or playing hard to forget. I'm lucky on this Antipodean island where no one has to wear a mask to the supermarket and we can afford to be slow with rolling out vaccinations until we can't. I shouldn't be looking elsewhere, but America remembers the island where I grew up. She's been drunk at KVI Beach, skinny dipping in the summer-cold Puget Sound. She's sat in my childhood kitchen, tripping on acid, while we spooned cookie dough onto baking trays. I'm back in Sydney lockdown now, planes still grounded. America said we'd have a festival-reunion when I make it back—all of our friends, camping—but she's gone off the rails and we're no longer talking. I know she's sick, angry at herself. My sister has a room waiting and I'm keeping an eye on flights, but memory is just fantasy and the ocean has never seemed so wide.

Patron Saint of Keeping House

The most revered angel of the twenty-first century and you don't even know I exist. I've washed your dishes, dropped your kids at school, fed your chickens, slept with you. Don't worry, your wife knows: she calls me. I drop into her body while she sublets a room down the coast. She stares out the window at rocky shorelines, and drinks her way through pots of Earl Grey, takes a bath and walks the hard-sand beach. Sometimes only a weekend, sometimes years.

Sanctuary

The fridge followed her home and sat on the doorstep. It was a vintage model with rounded edges and one door, the freezer set inside. Her husband said it would have to go or be put to use. Fair enough, it blocked the entryway—anyone arriving or leaving had to squeeze past. So she asked around the neighbourhood, took a photo and made copies. Found: one loved food-cooling unit. No takers. It waited patiently—always empty, beautifully clean. Then the washing machine turned up. This was spick, 1600 rpms and front-end loading. Not that it mattered, parked out on the driveway without a hook-up. In the evenings, she'd lean against its white shell and watch the fridge—the air crisp with the smell of wet grass, a belt of stars overhead. She began staying outside later and later until she woke one morning, neck sore. A blender and vacuum cleaner had appeared, propped against the fridge. And beyond, the lawn was packed with dryers and deep freezers, ovens and dishwashers, all of them perched like giant metal birds.

Costco: the (a)isle of the Lotus-Eaters

i.

Odysseus with his hipster beard drops you off in front of the roller doors. Get in, get out, he says—you need more Ciconian wine for tonight's house party. You dodge the packed trolleys, flashing your membership card. It's easy to scoff the consumerism but it takes restraint to walk past the triple-packs of gummy worms and mega-trays of cheese scrolls. Congratulate yourself until you catch sight of the lotus flowers. Free samples: deep-fried petals dipped in chocolate, swirls of peanut butter cream. Your hand reaches out. A tiny bite. And then, without warning, you've got hold of the tray. Shoppers jostle behind you and a fight's breaking out but all you can feel is sugar spiking your blood stream as you sink to the linoleum, drowsy, cream smeared on your face.

ii.

Odysseus journeys the aisles of Costco, surrounded by stuff that's also tired of travelling. Maple syrup shipped from America, dried apricots from Turkey, frozen berries from China and coffee beans from Colombia.

iii.

During lockdown, Odysseus isn't allowed to dock at port. He's trapped on the Ruby Princess, isolating in his cabin, while I stand in front of the pantry, finishing the last of the apricots, envious of how they've journeyed the world.

THE ONLY MAMMALS CAPABLE OF FLIGHT

I'm in the backyard of a house I share with my husband. The bats live under a bridge two suburbs away. They're large: fruit bats, the kind that make Gotham believable and daily life a dark cartoon. The first time they appear, I'm standing on the back step, bare feet on rounded concrete. I shout a sound that could be mistaken for 'hello', and they dive through neighbours' trees, past soccer goal and clothesline, heedless and unstoppable. The next night, I'm stretched out on a picnic blanket when dark settles. They come in ones and twos and then that steady thrum, taking over sky with chatter, conversation I can almost understand; and again, it feels like I matter. They're talking to deeper places, and I'm not fixed in this human body. Their black streak becomes a nightly pilgrimage, and I take to sleeping outside. No blankets or sheets, my frame exposed on that tartan cloth. Sometimes I climb a tree, hang by my knees. My husband pretends he doesn't notice but webbing grows between my arms and torso. Work is also a concern. Thank God for Covid—I can hide under a poncho for online meetings. I still walk with friends, but they worry about me and I nod. Denial is pointless: it is worrying. I no longer know what I am. Of course, it's inevitable—the bats stop coming. I don't cry but I stand at the kitchen sink, staring into the backyard. I sing to every hard-news love song I can find. I pound my furry chest until it bruises. They are bats, I remind myself. Bats. But my eyesight is shot and I dream only of horizons.

Terminal Four, LAX (I)

Watch your step, the stewardess says as I leave the aircraft. The jet-bridge has been cobbled together from defunct walkways and left-over airport parts, and I wonder if I've made some greater, unnameable mistake in disembarking. Night infects the accordion tunnel, and my shadow lacks proportion—but of course I'm wearing two masks, glasses, a face shield: we've all forgotten how to interpret the world.

Inside the transit lounge, and already I'm lost. No signs overhead, we could be in any generic waiting room—nothing signals 'airport'. People push around me, all of us hollow in the fluorescence, and I smell cigarettes and deodorant through clenched breath. We're in a psychic holding cell: the past two years a crowded room I'm not allowed to leave. I need to find Meghan. Again, I check my watch.

To my left, another line—a woman in a cheerful uniform behind a desk. International? I ask. She watches my face like I'm speaking a foreign language. Maybe I am. Someone behind me says I need Terminal Four. Another passenger's nodding towards the open glass where a shuttle waits, doors open. The driver powers up and we sit thigh-against-thigh, luggage at our feet, when my phone pings with a map request. Meghan is a blue dot in a parking garage, inching towards a large rectangle. I'm weaving over runways, around airplanes. When the bus arrives, everyone releases through the doors, a shared exhalation.

I text Meghan—Just got a shuttle to Terminal Four. She writes back—I thought that's where you were arriving. She's right, that's where I was supposed to land. Covid, the transit lounge, the lost two years: where have I been?

Optimism

My mother prayed for her plane to crash but I have more respect for flight—the momentum and fuel needed to launch cabin, wing and passenger. This cargo hold is packed with twenty years of us: that first group-house, your night shifts, the trip to hospital after fifteen hours of labour. When oxygen masks fall from the ceiling, I unbuckle my seatbelt, and lurch towards the cockpit: pilot seat empty, needles spin on the dash. I settle behind the controls and we catch a moment of calm like an air current, but altitude is dropping and the ground seems so certain. Landing comes quick, wheels smashed into fuselage—still, we're alive, teetering along a runway zigged with giant cracks and weeds. The airport is abandoned, overgrown with jungle and sunlight. It'll take some work but we can live in re-purposed planes like shipping containers—open-plan the cabins, renovate galleys into kitchens. We'll set up a few gates from each other; and on Sunday nights, I'll invite you over for dinner and we'll laugh and tell stories with survivors from other flights.

Self-Restraint

I watch from the window. The zombies are drilling and hammering with alluring industry. It looks like a ramp, maybe a skate park. Yes, they've built a skate park in the driveway next door. Scooters, boards—eight, nine, ten zombies slice along concrete, spill onto road, but no one cares, no one's parked here in months. The zombies go shopping and won't wear face masks. They come home with cases of beer and extra packs of toilet paper, laughing as they high-five each other, palm against palm. I haven't touched anyone in months now. Tonight they bring couches and armchairs out to the street and erect a screen at the end of the block so the cul de sac is now an outdoor cinema. Someone has ordered pizza. The zombies drink beer and make toasts, shouting over each other as opening credits begin. I hover on the porch, holding my coat—I love this movie—but someone coughs and I retreat. It's well past midnight now and they're running up and down the road, shrieking and whooping. I peek through curtains, hand pressed against glass, as they fall on the verge in front of my house, giggling and making out.

When We Could Travel—Dim Sum

The meals: sometimes I guzzle tea to keep from gagging and then I'm surprised by raw dough with sesame seed paste. Beautiful. The green bean ice water dessert is bizarre and gritty, unpleasant. Chicken claws outstretched on a plate. Then fried dough that's like eating fairy ribbons. But I'm stumped at the thousand-year-old egg. It's been marinated in dirt. The yolk is black, the egg-white amber. I only know it's an egg because my new friend is telling me so. You must try it, she says.

I'm not an adventurous eater. I've surprised myself so far—but this is too much. I know me. The egg won't make it from fork to mouth.

She leans close, hair pinned back in elaborate twists. I used to eat it as a child, every two weeks, she says. I understand: food is culture, culture is people, the person in front of me is her. I push the fork into my mouth, the marinated egg that is both egg and not-egg. It's salty, with traces of tea and yolk. Not unpleasant. She watches as I swallow. My fork reaches down again. I have no idea who I am.

Self-medication

At the supermarket, you haven't made it past the trolleys and you're yelling at your partner. Half the problem, at least, must be yours, so you sign up for online yoga and start getting up at 6am. Your downward dog is creaky, blind and stiff but you persevere. Doesn't make sense—stretching and silence, that's all—but now you can appreciate the hum of traffic, the smell of freshly cut grass. Then they're talking about redundancies at work and you're up at five-thirty, then five. Your grey-blue mat on the floorboards, your reflection in the windows. This helps, but your father gets sick and now it's four am. The tax bill is late: three. Sleep is overrated, you tell yourself, legs lifting for a headstand. When you've mastered wheel pose, your sessions are starting before midnight and it's only a matter of time before you're rolling out the mat when everyone else climbs into bed.

Travel Tip

I like travel but it takes forty-seven emails with the agent to purchase a plane ticket. I arrive four hours early to the airport and worry-bead the gates, connections and immigration checkpoints. Every plane I board is waiting to explode with terrorist righteousness, which I understand—we are decadent—but even adrenalin gets tired.

I've learned to lay my clothes out the night before, roller-bag by the door, and slip out to the street to the train to the airport before I wake.

Baggage Claim

We've landed at IKEA Airport. Our flights were on-time, luggage made it—my black roller bag filled with childhood driveways and dinner-table arguments and notions of what a living room ought to look like. We step off the escalator and I've got the baby strapped to my chest. You're half a pace ahead, marching past fictional bedrooms and I'm wondering at the kinds of people who'd make love in those beds and whether any of them might be me. You hoist up your red backpack—it's fraying at the straps and weighs a ton. The baby is sleeping as we pass kitchens with granite and timber benchtops. I've got a list in my purse, but when we finally make it downstairs we're too tired and the baby's crying and there're so many picture frames to choose from. In the cafeteria, we nab a window table and the baby nurses as I watch planes take off, consistent angles against the blue. Then salmon and meatballs and refillable cups of cola, and we're ready for departures. We hoist our luggage up onto the conveyor belt with the dining trays, but my roller bag catches on the plastic flaps and the flight attendant tells us protocol has changed, we have to carry our own luggage now.

Awards

My son received an award today and it felt like I was receiving an award for raising a child who receives awards. Leaving the school grounds, parents stopped us on the footpath, holding my arm, leaning close. But if I could choose an award—any award—it would be from my son's father and it would say: 'Award for not yelling' and he would present it to me three, four, five times a day. Our domestic life would become an ongoing series of ceremonies with the home appliances—toaster, vacuum cleaner, iron and kettle—lined up, applauding.

Domesticity

My Samsung front loader is a hamster wheel. I climb inside, running and running. But even so, the laundry is never finished.

Mother(land)

I woke early to write this morning and discovered zebras in the living room—they were chewing on the couch and scratching against the coffee table. I stepped around them, on my way to the study, but they were still there after drafting and morning wake-ups, after showers and cereal and double-checking the home reader was signed and packed into the school bag. Our son stared but I bundled him down the hallway, out the door, already late for my 8.30am. When we came home that afternoon, they'd moved into the kitchen. Of course you weren't worried. They'll move on, you said.

When night fell, I was washing dishes and they kept nuzzling my hand. I followed their uneven line off the veranda, past the newsagent, behind the post office. It was just a walk through town, nothing to keep secret. But we were home before daylight and it didn't come up over breakfast.

The next night the zebras were antsy and we left straight away, following train tracks up north, edging towards desert, and when darkness began to lift, I was staring at the endless red. In the distance I saw Charmian Clift on a tiger, unmistakeable in cowboy boots; and George Sand perched atop an elephant, laughing with Adrienne Rich; and Deborah Levy, of course she was there, running amidst a flock of deer.

Note to self:

Don't fill your thermos with red wine for the school picnic.

Last Day of Term

It's a parade of cars and a sidewalk of teachers. They're standing three metres apart. Some wear Book Week costumes, others hold streamers. I've taken turns being in love with all of them—the kindergarten teacher, now principal, with platforms and big hair; the Trekkie brainiac my son had for years three and five; the sports-lover in running shorts from year two. They're all waving while cars honk and children lean out of windows. My son begs me to stop crying but my head is dizzy and the seat belt has locked me in. We pause at the crosswalk on this suburban street, windscreen glittered with dust and sunlight, so faraway-close to normal it makes my chest hurt.

I'd like to Submit an Application

I'm a bit old for the position, maybe too much experience, but I think I'd fit into your team. I love the work environment. That wide front door and open plan kitchen—granite benchtops, breakfast bar. And the covered, outside dining: company personnel could fit around that table. I'm not a fan of the American flag nor the trophy gun, but every work site has things to be overlooked. You should have a copy of my resume, and of course you can contact my references. I'm looking for a change: I'm tired of adulting and you already have five sons. I don't think one more child would be too much bother—I'd pick up after myself, play Chopin on your piano in the entryway. I realise it could get a little complicated having a mother ten years younger than me and colleagues born last year, but just think how lovely for you both to have a girl.

Birthday Party

It will be fun. You, so committed to this fun, will raise your voice and speed through stoplights for last-minute ice. You will print colouring-in flags that cater for every guest's nationality and organise tiny potted plants as leaving gifts. The cake will be six storeys, each layer another colour of rainbow. But all of these heroic displays will fail, no matter how much fun is had or how many children pass the parcel—because this love you're celebrating is an animal howling in a hospital ward with no place in the backyard sun.

ACCEPTANCE

i.

Your husband sits on the couch, watching cricket. You're stranded on the living room floor with garbage bags of baby clothes. Your son is now in primary school and you can't figure out what's for the Salvos and what goes straight in the bin. You hold up a stained onesy. Your husband glances over. 'Bin.' Then a sweater. 'Salvos.' You reach for another, and he sighs, gaze pulling back to the screen, and you hate him for leaving you alone with all of those tiny sweaters you'll never need again.

ii.

Your husband sits on the couch, watching cricket. You're stranded on the living room floor with garbage bags of baby clothes. You're tired of sorting them alone so you grab a beer from the fridge and plonk beside him. When the next ad break arrives the bags have multiplied, piled on the floor, balanced on the table. School uniforms, soccer jerseys. When Australia declares, they line the hallway and crowd onto the kitchen bench—graduation gowns, fancy dress costumes—and before the afternoon has finished, you can't get to the door and your son is studying overseas and issuing wedding invitations.

but Wolf-girl in her gingham dress won't stop with the tantrums. She starts between my ribs, fist-paws against the glass of my chest. Then she's up and running in circles around my gut before I banish her outside. It's the howling I can't stand; what will the neighbours think? She's following me now. I cancelled tonight's party, said we were sick, who knows, maybe we are. We went through the drive-through for PCR tests and she relaxed in the car, hung her head out the window. But back home she started pacing the hallways: wanting to be fed, let out—how am I supposed to know? Sometimes I want to grab her by the snout and shake, but that just makes everything worse. The only thing that helps is when I rest a hand on her neck and remind her to breathe. Count to four, hold, release—we'll be okay, I'm looking after you.

Call an Ambulance

Life-as-we-knew-it was approached in an elevator by two assailants—baggy t-shirts, bandanas and hi-tops. They got on at the fifth floor, calling each other names too crass for the middle of the afternoon. When Life tried to step aside, the one with the goatee nudged back. Something didn't feel right, of course it didn't, but doors were already closing. Life stared at the ground, aware of the skinny one rubbing at his arms. And just when the elevator got some traction, just when it seemed things might be fine, Goatee with the bruised eye socket jammed a key into the panel and everyone shuddered to a halt.

Round Trip

The plane ticket arrived during Covid—a long, thin envelope in the mailbox, my name printed on the outside. It was one of those old ones, departures and arrivals layered on top of each other in red and blue ink. But there was no travelling then—only chartered flights for stranded citizens. Had to be a joke. Even so, I didn't tell anyone, kept the ticket locked in my desk. The flight left in eight weeks, and I didn't recognise the destination. I'd forget about it: life was fine. But, of course, I wasn't sleeping then, and I'd tiptoe to the study, slide key into drawer, make sure it was still there.

A month passed, and I was checking my desk three, four times a day. I'd stopped sleeping in my bed: instead, curling up in that high-backed leather chair.

4am of the flight, and I caught the train. A change of clothes in my roller bag, a mask over my face, I sat alone at the back of the carriage. No one else on board. At the airport, the ticket counters were unmanned, shops dimmed—a ghost terminal. I moved through security, taking my laptop out of the bag, placing shoes and belt in the blue plastic tray, but I could have walked straight through. Alone at the gate, I stopped waiting for my row to be called and shuffled down the ramp. No flight attendants as I stepped on board, but I found my seat. Belt clicked into place; cabin eerie as the aircraft pulled out; no voice from the captain. When the plane lifted, I stared through plexiglass at the dark. If I know anything, I can say this: we flew in a straight line, no dips or angles. No turbulence. But when we landed, I disembarked at the same terminal I'd just left.

Back home, I slid key into front door and kicked off my shoes, house quiet. I tiptoed from room to room, watching from each threshold—everyone was still sleeping.

I Don't Regret Anything

Usually I can't be bothered with the dishwasher but, with Covid in the house, extra-hot water's another safety measure. So I open the door to that exhalation of wet steam and pull out the top rack. In the corner, that red teacup I bought at the gallery. A Friday night and you and I were texting on that walk into town, my son ahead on his scooter, the night-streets awake with recent rain and traffic lights: everything giddy and alive. I took photos at the exhibition—no people, just artworks—and folded them into messages like paper cranes. I think I knew I'd never see you, not in-person, but I bought the cup anyway because I wanted something that belonged to our conversation. It's ceramic, no handle, with an imperfect lip that's almost oval, red glaze with white fronds, but you only see them if you take the time to look. Mostly, I don't. Mostly I don't even see you in the cup. But the memory of that night still warms the porcelain like morning coffee.

Domestic Gallery

i.

We're perched in front of a computer screen. I'm closer to the camera, out of proportion beside you. She appears in another square, this therapist I call Covid. Her methods are unconventional—an elimination diet of everything social to see what remains. You attend supermarkets like church now. I've worn through three pairs of shoes walking the 5km perimeter of what is possible.

ii.

We're perched in front of a computer screen. I'm closer to the camera, out of proportion beside you. She appears in another square, this therapist I call Covid. She asks what we want, and I concentrate on her blue sea-shell background—it bleeds onto her shoulders and arms. Now she asks what we want if we can't have what we want, and I wish I could blur into the background. Maybe I could become the bookcase you built for my birthday or the sewing cupboard full of fabrics. You carted yards and yards of cloth in your oversized, red backpack. I remember unfolding that lighthouse pattern from Florida, sewing it into the quilt we once slept under. The therapist asks us to face each other—you're shy, I'm crying now—and I imagine us as an exhibit of every object we've shared, a private curation of kindness.

Storm Water

The weather app shows more news will be falling through the weekend. At least thirty-five millimetres of headline today—case numbers, foreign aggression, stock market—and that's before lunch. A river of information now runs down your street, the yard is submerged in reports and interviews, and you're sandbagging the front door.

Terminal Four, LAX (II)

I'm in a proper terminal now—with gates, and screens that list departures and arrivals. Relief, but my phone reception has dropped, and I have no idea where to go. I'm wearing too many jackets, aware of my heart as a pulsing object beneath the layers. Which way? I need a compass, stars. Then Meghan appears on-screen, and I show my phone to two women with security badges. One of them touches the glass, enlarging the map with artificial nails, before remembering and pulling back. She tells me to go straight. I'll have to leave the airport, re-enter security for my next flight. I nod and four minutes later: Meghan, me, our dots hover on top of each other but the corridor is full of strangers. A text: Go to baggage, downstairs. Backpack digs into my shoulders, legs cramp, but I'm running now, searching for stairs, until there, behind an empty information desk—an elevator. Inside, I press the button with my elbow, and stand in the centre. It feels like all four walls could be doors and when we stop moving, the one behind me opens.

Childcare

i.

You don't want to be left in that big room, walls covered in murals, with no idea of what to do or who to play with. The sad news is you will never grow out of this. When you arrive at parties, this same feeling will descend—but maybe you will remember: all those people dancing in the living room and sitting on kitchen countertops had to step over the threshold from not-party to party; every Self was once an arriving Other. One day we may marvel at this but right now we need to tuck your backpack into a cubby and sign you in, and your weeping exhausts me as though it's my face that's wet and swollen.

ii.

When you arrive at immigration, this same feeling will descend—but maybe you will remember: most of those people on the other side of customs (their parents, grandparents) were once arriving Others.

7.30AM

I look after children who are not mine, sometimes in the mornings before school. Their moods are like magpies circling the living room—all sharp beak and straight flight. I've taken to wearing a bicycle helmet decorated with cable ties, even inside.

Immigrant Glazier

i.

Suburban house, cul de sac. I'm standing in the backyard where it's dark, and sliding glass reflects: no one inside can see me—they're cooking roasts in the middle of summer and sunbathing at Bondi and napping in front of the television during the Boxing Day Test. Behind me, the high school band marches onto a football field, killer whales arc through Puget Sound and even highschoolers dress up for Halloween. I stand so close to the pane for so many years my molecules make way for the silicon dioxide until I am part of the glass, rigid and reflective, not one side or the other but both at the same time.

ii.

I am sliding-door glass, rigid and reflective, cold winter at my back. Australian sun and open sky inside as my son launches mountain bike over fridge, landing on countertop, skidding past sink. On his surfboard, he paddles, catching a wave down that slope of armchair, disappearing into floorboards. I hold my breath until he surfaces, laughing, so comfortable and committed to the great indoors.

Time Travel

Postcards keep arriving, asking me to visit—I think I'm ready. My suitcase is vintage 1970s. A muted sea-blue rectangle of Samsonite with silver edging and a plastic handle. Utterly graceful, despite its size, with four little wheels on the bottom and latches that pop out. Everything's folded inside—regular sleep, meditation, daily exercise, lots of vegetables. The therapist-cum-travel agent is confident with our itinerary, but I keep opening the case and combing through that gathered pocket, afraid I am forgetting something.

Avian Influenza

Sometimes she gets in the car and drives in circles around the neighbourhood—windows sealed—screaming at sky, while a tiny chicken pecks at her heart.

Your Poem is a Plane Flight

for Lydia Davis

One stanza, less than a page, and I'm running through the terminal, boarding slip and passport ready. Only twelve lines so I'm quick, sinking into my aisle seat as doors close. Alliteration and enjambment, the imperative dictated by a comma. The language is mostly Anglo-Saxon, except for the word 'remain'. What remains: both question and statement. I fasten my seatbelt. The rhythm slows. Outside oval windows, night falls and one-by-one everyone pulls down their blinds. A final couplet. It will be okay: the pilot understands. This loneliness has company. Pilot, poet: we share the dark, new skies.

Hope

There are different levels to this grief, like cloudbanks in the sky, but if you keep climbing, way up, the sun shines and air is bright. Look, over there: a kamikaze pilot who's forgotten her fear of heights.

Flight

There's Covid in the high rise and I'm on the top floor. They wear hazmat suits to deliver groceries and I'm not allowed to leave. Swallows nest under the eaves and fly in anxious arcs. I envy their mobility.

I set up cameras and live-stream birds to the internet. Something to do—nesting, babies, spring. In the live feed chat: Birdlove71 from Arcata, California, likes the dual perspectives. I write back with too much enthusiasm about the geometry of wing spans. He sends photos of an acorn woodpecker, spotted in his yard—red skullcap, shimmery black-blue feathers.

We watch the swallows for days; sometimes there's a green dot beside his name, we're both online. Mostly, he messages when I'm asleep and I respond in the early mornings, sitting at my window with a cup of strong coffee. It occurs to me the birds could be born at night and so I order an infrared camera—Birdlove's relieved, I can tell—but we don't need it. They arrive in late afternoon.

Birdlove71:	It's happening. The hatchlings.
SwallowSolitude:	I've never seen this. Not live.

The egg is white with brown spots. A long, thin crack starts at the top and moves down until the shell splits open, claws and beak scrambling. Then, a pink, gelatinous body emerges with a weird, huge head—blind circles for eyes. Everything about the creature yearns upwards. I'm watching the screen. Of course, it's right there, other side of the window, but I can't pull away from the extreme close-up.

SwallowSolitude: Hypnotic.
Birdlove71: Vulnerable.

There are four babies. Mother and father swoop—disappearing, returning—and the young guzzle food from their beaks. One fledgling seems silly, self-deprecating. Another, bookish. Maybe it's the ruffle of their new feathers.

Birdlove71: Sometimes, watching them, I forget I'm human.

I know this feeling—it comes at night. I slide open the window and perch on its ledge, all feather and delicate bone. With an exhalation, I drop onto currents. The air is cold, glinting with tiny insects. I dip down. In the next block of apartments, I watch a woman through her window; she's wearing a shawl, face cast in television-blue shadows. In the park, a couple walk their dog. Then I climb above rooftops, and follow the freeway with those relentless tail lights.

Birdlove sends photos of fish tacos. I send famous poems I'm not sure I like. He tells me his wife died last year, they're still waiting to hold the memorial. I tell him of my mother's dementia and the cleaner who brings her liquorice, the email updates assuring me all staff have been vaccinated. Birdlove works too hard, his son—newly returned to school—keeps losing coats. I admit I'm afraid the world is ending.

Birdlove71: Or beginning.

The next morning, the nest is empty.

Birdlove71: Where are they? Have they fallen?

I'm not thinking. I jolt down the stairwell in my bathrobe. Can't wait for the elevator. I've seen the front of my building on the news—all of the security guards enforcing lockdown—but the foyer is empty, ghostlike, and I rush through the automatic glass doors. The concrete is blank. Oh, thank God. I stand in the morning sun, heat on my neck, staring up at the blue.

Seasons

You skip stones across the lake of my chest. There's a wooden rowboat, and you like the sturdy oars, arms pulling against the weight of water. In the middle, fish nip at the surface and you lay back, shoulder blades against hull, sun overhead. Onshore, evergreens are patient when you dock, watching the horizon for winter. It can arrive daily—ice, occasional snowdrifts. But you like the white outlines of tree against sky, and enjoy exercise: you're a graceful skater. Your legs move with purpose, hands loose at your sides. Easy turns, that gentle sway from side to side, your path etched and visible. And when it's too cold, you build a quiet fire on the shore to warm your hands.

Recognition

Little Red Riding Hood was on that uphill stretch in the darkest part of the forest, the smell of moss and fungus and damp hanging from the trees. Bit of bramble-rough catching on her cloak. She tiptoed over the ravine, balancing on the trunk of a dead tree and when she hopped down on the other side, Wolf was waiting. About time. She shrugged, hood dropping to the ground, all body hair and pricked ears. And Wolf gazed at her, fur gleaming, as the two circled each other, howling and grateful.

Equations of Goodness

Some people are more complicated than others. I am more complicated than you, but you are a better person. You wish I were a better person and in my complicated way, I work hard at my bettering, harder than you. Maybe I, then, am the better person. I say this and you laugh, though not unkindly. My mother, however, is more complicated than either of us and utterly unconcerned with being a good person.

Refuge

There's a woman sitting in a rocking chair, gazing out of my left eye. There's another woman in a hammock, strung between my ribs. She's trying to take a nap but there're more women in my left leg—grabbing milk from the corner shop, rushing to the post office—and their hurry is contagious. Sometimes all these women crowd around a long table in my forearm, but meals are exhausting. Too many in the kitchen, checking casseroles, interrupting each other. The woman in the rocking chair, she's taken her plate upstairs so she can eat alone with that eye-socket view over street—power lines relax in gentle curves above the footpath and neighbourhood kids have left their bicycles on the lawn again.

Compromise

His girlfriend lives underwater. He was hoping for a mermaid but squids aren't bad. She has eight arms that curl around him when they sleep, swaying with the tide. She's gentle, sometimes tentative—the slightest shadow and she retracts under her rocky outcrop. It takes a while for her to emerge through the barnacles and kelp, but he's okay waiting. The real bummer is the distance. She's comfortable on the seabed, where it's calm. Below the waves, there's no traffic, mortgages or supermarket lines. It irritates her, the way he's always swimming to the surface, gulping for air, or turning up in his waterlogged suit. But he makes compromises, too. She's got sea-breath: all those fish and crustaceans she eats. The insomnia and the colour-changing. But when night falls, her organs glow and he can watch her three hearts pulsing.

Reflection

I dreamed you from the screen and now I'm in your house, crouched in a stairwell with your ten-year-old son. We're holding Nerf guns—I've got a big one that can shoot rounds of twenty bullets and my pockets are packed with ammunition. We're up against you and your eldest, and we need to get to your base: down the stairs, around the corner and through the living room. You can see them, your ten-year-old says—in the reflection, look at the wedding picture of mom and dad. The portrait hangs at the bottom. I almost don't recognise you, both bride and groom staring at camera. She leans against you, but she's looking at me—an expression of quiet joy and disbelief, maybe. Her son beside me, both of us listening for movement. Get ready, he says. They're coming.

Interspecific Feeding

9am, Sunday morning. You push through the gate, unlock the oak door, and your mother's in the kitchen, making scrambled eggs and coffee that's either too strong or too weak. The computer screen, perched over the dining table, is already illuminated with your pixelated sister. Your father's hands rest on the clear plastic tablecloth and your mother sits beside him. It's your turn. There's been a job offer and you're wondering what we're meant to do with our time on this planet. You're worried about your boys and school, how much you should urge them to conform. And your lover, on the other side of an ocean. The more you talk, the more your feathers bristle against the lining of your jacket. Your sister nods as your nose turns beak, and no one exclaims when your head rotates full circle. Maybe they're used to it. When you pause, your sister tells of a church excursion and how much the ferry cost, and your mother wants to know how much rain to expect in the week. It's hard for you to answer because you're perched on the cupboard now, swooping in arcs over the table: you just missed your father's bald head.

We are Waking Up

Your message, the playlist. I watch a band tonight for the first time in over a year. Shoulder-to-shoulder—strangers bump into each other, my hand brushes a woman's waist. In front of the stage, a colleague: something's changed since we were in the office, more weight or the slope of shoulder, maybe. Lights cast yellow-orange while the saxophone radiates through an intoxicated fury of bodies. We know what it means now, to be pack animals. The girl in the restroom, toilet door open. The smell of vomit as she's walk-carried by a friend, black denim skirt caught on her waist, butt-cheek exposed—but now I'm on the dancefloor and the beat moves through me, and there's a voice that belongs to a singer who's wearing a pale slip that hugs her beautiful, sturdy thighs. She holds the microphone up on stage like a triumph and I want her to keep singing as long as I'm alive, but the show ends and the lights come up—remorse—and that song by Talking Heads comes on. You know the one. You posted it in that early message, a pre-emptive apology.

Double Luck

My girlfriend is falling apart. At first it was just a finger. She'd be writing the shopping list or playing the piano, and one might click out of place and go rolling under her chair. Then maybe an arm, a leg. Sometimes at restaurants, she'd stand for the bathroom, and the lopsidedness would send her tumbling with cutlery and water glasses. A little awkward, but we got used to it; I'd warn the waiters. My friends and parents were worried—what happens when she's driving? They don't understand: she's cobbled from factory seconds, it's lucky she's held together as long as she has. And I can't talk, I'm a bit worn too: my arms are different models, and I've got two left hands. Sometimes at night we trade limbs and hold each other—it's a funny feeling, my own arms around myself.

Terminal Four, LAX (III)

Elevator doors release and there she is, against a cement column. Meghan recognises me through the safety gear and we're running at each other until we're swaying. I pull back. Her hair is longer, face narrow. Car's this way, she says. We're outside the airport now, and the street feels empty and safe. I want to hold her hand but need to sanitise.

Decades ago, during summers in college, we worked in a bakery with sagging floorboards and wisteria hanging over windows. We'd sneak out through beaded curtains and scoop handfuls of cookie dough from the walk-in fridge. We drank so much coffee we were the most awake we'd ever be in our lives.

We're crossing traffic, walking into a parking garage. I lift face shield, mask: fresh air in my throat. Meghan beeps open her car and we're sitting in the front seats, faces naked, hands sticky, as she twists into a bottle of wine. The dashboard offers a picnic: cheese and cookies, bread and fruit. She pours cabernet sauvignon into stemless glasses and I'm remembering the first time I drank wine: the two of us, near KVI beach, we'd been collecting driftwood to make mobiles. She presses my arm. We don't have long, she says.

It takes a moment because I'm already crying. Not because I'm sad, though of course I'm sad, maybe it's the intimacy of climbing into her car. I choose the middle of the story and circle back until I spiral to the end and we're both crying. Time has slowed—two years in thirty minutes. Talking to her feels performative—the spoken word enacts. By articulating change to this woman, it now exists. Everyone is fundamentally good, I hear myself saying. That's what makes it heartbreaking.

Just like your mother, she muses, as though this were a compliment. The three of us used to get stoned during those summers, on the outside balcony where I grew up, overlooking the fir trees. I tell Meghan to shut up and we both laugh, and I feel my mother eating at the wallpaper inside my chest.

Reckoning

We're trudging through snow in bathrobes and rubber boots and brightly coloured beanies. This way, my mother says. I'm carrying the broom, following her over the criss-cross of deer tracks. It's a struggle for footing—powder, ice, and beneath that: home. I climbed into her bed last night. Sleeping with a lion, I thought, and had to tip-toe to the bathroom for small, white pills to relax into the flannel. Now she leads me past snow-heavy branches and clumps of bamboo, and we're almost there, the bright orange and blue house watching from the hill. Ready—she asks, reaching out, and I hand her the broom so she can shovel snow from the hot tub. Prayer flags hang over us, strung from the pagoda. And just beyond—tall, thin sculptures that remind me of Buddhist temples. She's talking about her ex-boyfriends now, and we're laughing, and I hear my voice like my chest is this valley and the air holds laughter like ice crystals. It's been a long time and I can't help forgiving her if it means this feeling in my rib cage. The hot tub is ready now and she's popping the lock, pulling back the cover for that rush of steam.

THE THERAPIST ISN'T HAPPY WITH US

Our son sleeps in the living room. Sometimes in the kitchen while he's baking cookies. He sleeps on top of the house, balanced on red tiles, curled around chimney. Or on his bicycle riding up the mountain. He sleeps playing soccer and shouting at his friends during computer games and then again when he checks my king in chess. He sleeps sometimes in my bed, mostly in yours, and it's very wrong, this behaviour. We're not teaching him to be independent, this child who can navigate Heathrow and cook dinner and make his own way to school.

Insect Wisdom

I was gripped with manuscript panic, so I ventured into the backyard for perspective and sunlight. Three paces from the door, a giant bug swooped. It was five metres across, prehistoric, all wings and fang, ant-beetle-wasp. I was caught between pincers, hung upside-down. You stood on the stoop, arms crossed. Our son waved, eyeing off the antennas and bulbous eyes. You sighed, ushering him to the car for his trombone lesson and dinner at yours while I stayed suspended above grass. Days passed. Weeks. The neighbour's dog finally shut up. And when I too accepted my precarity, the fierce grip around my torso relaxed and I toppled to the ground.

Knowledge > Rest

He doesn't have a bed—instead, his room is filled with back-to-back bookshelves like stacks in a library. It's a small house, but you must travel long corridors and stairwells to get to this bookroom, and then it's not certain you can return. I understand, but it's dark, even though there are windows, and the weary shelves remind me of tombs. How does he sleep, I wonder. Maybe he whispers himself thin as a bookmark and slides between the sheet-pages, dreaming with all the words and thoughts that have come before him.

One Use for Ladders

You stand on a ladder inside my chest, rungs lodged against my rib cage. You hold the steel wool in fist, arm overhead. Your hand moves in circles, scrubbing at my insides, and the motion moves through your shoulder blade. Now there's a sheen on your forehead, but you could go all day. Paint-speckled trousers, the whiff of work. You stop every now and then to assess your progress, while I'm hungry and dizzy with new-found clean, amazed by a view that's always been there.

Brain Coral

My wet-suit skin constricts until I tip back, off-boat. That splash of water and I'm mobile. I adjust my mask—that smell of brine, rubber—and context turns me miraculous: I breathe underwater, both heavy and weightless in the echoed silence. Reefs stretch below. Fish and crustaceans dart through red-pink spines. Sponges and sea turtles current-drift. And below: that coral ecosystem—one tiny exo-skeleton at a time, growing on top of ancestor fossils. But there are reef worlds, deeper than this, existing in near-complete darkness. Species that live in trenches, beneath acidic waters and bleaching, might just survive.

Perhaps our brains are reefs. Perhaps our survival, too, depends on dropping deeper—breathing into presence, below waves, into quiet.

Negotiations

i.

He has fallen in love with a barnacle attached to the bottom of a great ship. The barnacle is an arthropod, sharp but humble, very committed. Unfortunately, the ship is never docked long. Its captain, Wolf-girl, cackles in the bridge and pulls from shore on a whim. She orders engines to full, scraping past boats and smashing into ports. The barnacle is tired of these adventures, and dreams of releasing Wolf-girl and the ship, free-floating with plankton and jellyfish. Maybe this love, maybe he will join her as a barnacle and they can hold fast onto a blue whale, discover the oceans of the world.

ii.

He has fallen in love with a barnacle attached to the bottom of a great ship. Its captain is exhausting and unruly, so barnacle drops from the vessel and takes hold of whale. Her love joins, but Wolf-girl begs to come too. Surprisingly, she doesn't cause much fuss now. She rides up top, enjoying the view and holding onto sleek whale-skin, and they content themselves beneath, fastened to the underbelly of this giant creature.

Longing Distance

Birds cross screen-text seas, urged by the call of dry land. Those three thinking dots hold the falconer's gaze, while a fishing boat rocks on waves.

Saint Christopher

I book seats 16A and B. You book 16D, E and F. Our children will have known each other a week. I imagine soccer and Wordle and raised eyebrows about how other households do things. What about C, I ask? Whoever sits there will have to become part of our family; they'll have no choice. It's a joke, but family has become elastic. There is no C, you say. The plane is five seats across. But there's always a 16C, I think. Even if it's aisle, even if no one knows it's there. I picture the blue paisley upholstery and drop-down seat tray, the buttons for downlights and steward call. It dawns on me, of course, the seat is already taken—I don't believe spirits haunt the living, but your wife will sit beside me, hold my hand as we take off, and the journey will feel protected and safe.

Trojan Trophy

The first time they had sex—after texts and songs and video calls when she couldn't stop laughing—he rolled back and stared at the paint peeling around those sculpted architraves. She was asleep, naked on top of the sheet, rib cage rising and falling. Something, maybe a handle, no a door, definitely a door, appeared just above her hip, about the size of a large matchbox. He pressed it, rapped against timber. She let out a sleep-sigh but eyes didn't open. Then another door, stainless steel, on her neck. And more: on her calf, forearm, stomach. Some were carved, others plain. Some had bolts and delicate keyholes and plates of stained glass. They were impressive, the craftsmanship alone, but odd. Definitely odd. He should wake her, he thought, make sure she's okay, but just as he reached over, all of the handles turned and hundreds of Greek warriors came rushing out—ready to destroy her or him, he didn't know.

Unrequited

He drops pennies down her wishing-well throat. She could choke with these pocket-worn desires. But she laughs and they keep falling, never landing—her chest, a wish-limbo.

Someone high up (maybe God?) has made an administrative error. You can't possibly leave the maternity ward. Not today. Maybe not for years, if ever. You check on the baby even though he's right beside you—asleep, still breathing. Someone will have to bring clothes, of course. More books would be nice. But you're resigned—they told you everything would change and now here you are. Carve out a niche around the bed. Remember to ask for your patchwork quilt from home. And your dining table, that would look lovely tucked up against the beige wall. You could sit there with the nice nurse from California or the mother-of-twins. There's time. You'll be here until your son starts university or an apprenticeship (his life, his decisions). But they can't expect you to keep this thing alive on your own. Surely not.

Joy, Love, You

The bird on the power line waits. I didn't understand I could join him on that black wire, that I could push off from the kitchen window and afford myself an aerial perspective of this borrow-sugar, carpool-kids, weekend-drinks neighbourhood. That I could trust my wing-scapula, that it is possible to navigate using the verticality of height instead of the plane of horizons, that high voltage can be safe but only if you release the ground.

Tea Break

We take turns diving into the teapot. I'm wearing a retro swimsuit and a bathing cap. You're in Hawaiian boardshorts. I stand with toes lined up on the ceramic lip, back curved, arms outstretched. The water's high so there's not much time before I'll hit surface, but I'm careful anyways, building nerve. Of course you can't help yourself, you run up along the porcelain handle and leap—arms wrapped around legs, head tucked—drenching me with English Afternoon.

Generosity

It's a superhero collective—Cat/Bat/Wonder/Super Woman. They've all jumped story to walk out of this burning building. It's an abandoned house, single-story with a detached garage, on the far end of a cul-de-sac. Smoke billows behind them and the smell of petrol and burning timber hangs in the air. It's been raining and that makes everything glisten. The women are lined up elbow-to-elbow, each step in magnified tandem. The sky has no clouds, but no stars, either, and the concrete is lined with cracks. You watch this, cartoon or cinema—it could be either—and you're looking for me. I'm the real hero, you know that. But I'm not flanked, with confident posture, I'm the building, the one going up in flames. I'm about to explode, but I waited. Don't you see? I got them out. They're going to do glorious things and their whole lives are ahead of them and I waited to let everything blow to smithereens.

Brothers

My son and I aren't expecting it, but of course the museum is famous for this painting: all I remember is traipsing among Georgia O'Keefe's flowers and skulls when I was exactly his age. We catch an elevator, press the button—a family joins us, two brothers wrestling the tiny perimeter, bumping into me. When we're released into the foyer, an open doorway leads to a room with a crowd in front of a painting that looks very much like Vincent Van Gogh's Starry Night. That's not real, is it, my son asks? I think it might be, I say. We have a postcard of this painting on the bathroom wall, a postcard I must have bought in this very museum during the fog of my son's early infancy. Everyone is holding up phones, layers of screens at attention, and I cannot help taking photos of people taking photos. Spectators move in and out of frame, letting me shift closer to the artwork, until I'm there, directly in front of it, making eye-contact with the glowing moon. It's the brushstrokes that bring me undone—gentle, small arcs, painted by a hand that belonged to a man who was real, and he was able to paint this illuminated landscape because he had a brother who cared for him, financed him. And I understand, maybe for the first time in my life, that great artworks and novels and scores are not created by individuals. I'm crying now. This devotion of brothers is big as a night-sky cathedral and makes me think of my son's father, another man who cares for a brother afflicted with visions. A father who would have been here with us, admiring this painting, if I'd been able to love in a different way.

Visiting

I saw my dead mother yesterday like she'd driven through time. She was stopped in city traffic, the car ahead of me. A bright blue 1970s Cortina 1600—squat, with bench seats and a side column shift. Her best friend from high school sat beside her. Both of them had long hair, pulled back with feathers. My mother was talking, one hand in the air, telling a joke or a story. Laughing. A piece of coral hung from the rear-view mirror between them.

My mother's right arm rested on the open window frame. I stared at her profile. She was wearing glasses, the same ones she wore in high school photos taken just before I was born. She reached down to the radio and began shifting the dial.

I thought of leaving my car, walking through the traffic lanes and knocking on the back door to be let in. I thought of pulling her from the car and refusing to let go, refusing to step aside even when horns blared from behind us. I was thinking of how tiny she'd been in that hospital bed—the steel rail, the too-small sheets—and how I'd climbed up beside her, afraid of crushing her. And then the lights turned, and the Cortina moved forward, changing lanes, rounding the corner towards the heart of the city before I could follow.

Terminal Four, LAX (IV)

If Covid's blown my life apart, Meghan's has solidified. Parenthood, work, a husband who refuses to get vaccinated, her longing for an artistic practice. She empties the bottle into my glass—I just have to be sober enough to get through security and find my gate. I check the time: of course I want more than an hour and a half with this woman, but already the ceding ritual of mask, glasses, face shield. I take a deep breath, opening the car door, and Meghan walks me across the parking lot to security. We hug at the glass and I keep turning around. She's waving and I'm waving back, both of us laughing until I round the corner to the conveyor belts.

When I board the flight to Australia, the plane is only half-full and I have three seats to myself. The steward hands out sanitised blankets and headphones, and I wipe down the seat tray, buckling myself in as the captain's voice sounds through the cabin. When lights dim, we pull from the gate, and taxi towards runway. It must be our turn now because we're rushing forward, faster and faster, until that strange moment that feels like a pause and wheels lift.

Multiple Lifetimes. Not Serially, Though. Simultaneously.

Maybe it's core to the immigrant, restlessness and imagining. But this desire is bigger than 'path' and 'not-taken'. I want both and I want to be the whole woods, too—every fern, tree and canopy, the ground underfoot, the smell of composting leaves and arriving rain.

Flight
by Shady Cosgrove

This book was written on the traditional lands of the Dharawal, Yuin and Wadi Wadi people. I pay respects to their Elders, past, present and emerging, and to all First Nations people.

Acknowledgement is made to the following publications in which some of these poems first appeared: *Remnants*, Spineless Wonders, 2024; *Dreaming Awake*, MadHat Press, 2023; *The Writing Mind*, Recent Work Press, 2023; *Antipodes*, Vol 36, Issue 1, 2022; *Play*, Spineless Wonders, 2022; *The Road Not Taken*, Lee and Penn Publishing, 2022; *Eunoia Review*, 2021; *The Incompleteness Book II*, Recent Works Press, 2021; *Pulped Fiction*, Spineless Wonders, 2021; *SCAN Science/Art Network Project*, 2021; *takahe*, The Takahe Collective Trust, 2021; *The Australian Anthology of Prose Poetry*, Melbourne University Press, 2020; *The Incompleteness Book*, Recent Works Press, 2020; *New Writing*, Volume 17, Issue 1, 2019; *Time*, Spineless Wonders, 2018; *Cordite*, Suburbia Issue, 2018; *Landmarks*, Spineless Wonders, 2017; *Out of Place*, Spineless Wonders, 2015; *Flashing the Square*, Spineless Wonders, 2014; *Small Wonder*, Spineless Wonders, 2012.

First published 2024

POETRY

ISBN: 978-0-6459209-6-3

BOOK, TYPESETTING, AND LOGO DESIGN
Mountains Brown Press

PUBLISHER
Life Before Man

Gazebo Books
PO Box 375
Summer Hill
New South Wales 2130
Australia

gazebobooks.com.au

This book was made possible thanks to Anthony Mark Day

COVER IMAGE: *Her No.1*, 2023, oil on canvas, 122 x 92 cm, © Phil Day

www.ingramcontent.com/pod-product-compliance
Lightning Source LLC
LaVergne TN
LVHW051005080826
845145LV00009B/2468

* 9 7 8 0 6 4 5 9 2 0 9 6 3 *